This Playbook Belongs To Coach:

Jared McMinn

Year/Season:

2020

MONTH:

SUN	MON	TUES	WED	THURS	FRI	SAT

MONTH:

SUN	MON	TUES	WED	THURS	FRI	SAT

MONTH:

SUN	MON	TUES	WED	THURS	FRI	SAT

MONTH:

SUN	MON	TUES	WED	THURS	FRI	SAT

MONTH:

SUN	MON	TUES	WED	THURS	FRI	SAT

MONTH:

SUN	MON	TUES	WED	THURS	FRI	SAT

MONTH:

SUN	MON	TUES	WED	THURS	FRI	SAT

MONTH:

SUN	MON	TUES	WED	THURS	FRI	SAT

MONTH:

SUN	MON	TUES	WED	THURS	FRI	SAT

MONTH:

SUN	MON	TUES	WED	THURS	FRI	SAT

MONTH:

SUN	MON	TUES	WED	THURS	FRI	SAT

MONTH:

SUN	MON	TUES	WED	THURS	FRI	SAT

GAME STATISTICS

DATE:_____   OPPONENT: _____ H/A

	1ST QTR	2ND QTR	3RD QTR	FINAL
US				
OPPONENT				

PLAYER	SOLO TACKLES	ASSISTS	TOTAL SACKS	QB SACKS	TACKLE LOSS	INT	FUMBLES CAUSED	FUMBLE RECOV.

PLAYER	SOLO TACKLES	ASSISTS	TOTAL SACKS	QB SACKS	TACKLE LOSS	INT	FUMBLES CAUSED	FUMBLE RECOV.
PLAYER	SOLO TACKLES	ASSISTS	TOTAL SACKS	QB SACKS	TACKLE LOSS	INT	FUMBLES CAUSED	FUMBLE RECOV.

41/51 Fast Screen

DIAGRAM 1

DIAGRAM 2

NOTES

DIAGRAM 1

DIAGRAM 2

NOTES

DIAGRAM 1

DIAGRAM 2

NOTES

GAME STATISTICS

DATE:_____   OPPONENT: _____ H/A

	1ST QTR	2ND QTR	3RD QTR	FINAL
US				
OPPONENT				

PLAYER	SOLO TACKLES	ASSISTS	TOTAL SACKS	QB SACKS	TACKLE LOSS	INT	FUMBLES CAUSED	FUMBLE RECOV.

PLAYER	SOLO TACKLES	ASSISTS	TOTAL SACKS	QB SACKS	TACKLE LOSS	INT	FUMBLES CAUSED	FUMBLE RECOV.
PLAYER	SOLO TACKLES	ASSISTS	TOTAL SACKS	QB SACKS	TACKLE LOSS	INT	FUMBLES CAUSED	FUMBLE RECOV.

DIAGRAM 1

DIAGRAM 2

NOTES

DIAGRAM 1

DIAGRAM 2

NOTES

DIAGRAM 1

DIAGRAM 2

NOTES

DIAGRAM 1

DIAGRAM 2

NOTES

GAME STATISTICS

DATE:_____   OPPONENT: _____   H/A

	1ST QTR	2ND QTR	3RD QTR	FINAL
US				
OPPONENT				

PLAYER	SOLO TACKLES	ASSISTS	TOTAL SACKS	QB SACKS	TACKLE LOSS	INT	FUMBLES CAUSED	FUMBLE RECOV.

PLAYER	SOLO TACKLES	ASSISTS	TOTAL SACKS	QB SACKS	TACKLE LOSS	INT	FUMBLES CAUSED	FUMBLE RECOV.

DIAGRAM 1

DIAGRAM 2

NOTES

DIAGRAM 1

DIAGRAM 2

NOTES

DIAGRAM 1

DIAGRAM 2

NOTES

DIAGRAM 1

DIAGRAM 2

NOTES

GAME STATISTICS

DATE:_____   OPPONENT: _____   H/A

	1ST QTR	2ND QTR	3RD QTR	FINAL
US				
OPPONENT				

PLAYER	SOLO TACKLES	ASSISTS	TOTAL SACKS	QB SACKS	TACKLE LOSS	INT	FUMBLES CAUSED	FUMBLE RECOV.

PLAYER	SOLO TACKLES	ASSISTS	TOTAL SACKS	QB SACKS	TACKLE LOSS	INT	FUMBLES CAUSED	FUMBLE RECOV.
PLAYER	SOLO TACKLES	ASSISTS	TOTAL SACKS	QB SACKS	TACKLE LOSS	INT	FUMBLES CAUSED	FUMBLE RECOV.

DIAGRAM 1

DIAGRAM 2

NOTES

DIAGRAM 1

DIAGRAM 2

NOTES

DIAGRAM 1

DIAGRAM 2

NOTES

DIAGRAM 1

DIAGRAM 2

NOTES

GAME STATISTICS

DATE:_____   OPPONENT: _____   H/A

	1ST QTR	2ND QTR	3RD QTR	FINAL
US				
OPPONENT				

PLAYER	SOLO TACKLES	ASSISTS	TOTAL SACKS	QB SACKS	TACKLE LOSS	INT	FUMBLES CAUSED	FUMBLE RECOV.

PLAYER	SOLO TACKLES	ASSISTS	TOTAL SACKS	QB SACKS	TACKLE LOSS	INT	FUMBLES CAUSED	FUMBLE RECOV.

DIAGRAM 1

DIAGRAM 2

NOTES

DIAGRAM 1

DIAGRAM 2

NOTES

DIAGRAM 1

DIAGRAM 2

NOTES

DIAGRAM 1

DIAGRAM 2

NOTES

GAME STATISTICS

DATE:_____ OPPONENT: _____ H/A

	1ST QTR	2ND QTR	3RD QTR	FINAL
US				
OPPONENT				

PLAYER	SOLO TACKLES	ASSISTS	TOTAL SACKS	QB SACKS	TACKLE LOSS	INT	FUMBLES CAUSED	FUMBLE RECOV.

PLAYER	SOLO TACKLES	ASSISTS	TOTAL SACKS	QB SACKS	TACKLE LOSS	INT	FUMBLES CAUSED	FUMBLE RECOV.
PLAYER	SOLO TACKLES	ASSISTS	TOTAL SACKS	QB SACKS	TACKLE LOSS	INT	FUMBLES CAUSED	FUMBLE RECOV.

DIAGRAM 1

DIAGRAM 2

NOTES

DIAGRAM 1

DIAGRAM 2

NOTES

DIAGRAM 1

DIAGRAM 2

NOTES

DIAGRAM 1

DIAGRAM 2

NOTES

GAME STATISTICS

DATE:_____   OPPONENT: _____   H/A

	1ST QTR	2ND QTR	3RD QTR	FINAL
US				
OPPONENT				

PLAYER	SOLO TACKLES	ASSISTS	TOTAL SACKS	QB SACKS	TACKLE LOSS	INT	FUMBLES CAUSED	FUMBLE RECOV.

PLAYER	SOLO TACKLES	ASSISTS	TOTAL SACKS	QB SACKS	TACKLE LOSS	INT	FUMBLES CAUSED	FUMBLE RECOV.
PLAYER	SOLO TACKLES	ASSISTS	TOTAL SACKS	QB SACKS	TACKLE LOSS	INT	FUMBLES CAUSED	FUMBLE RECOV.

DIAGRAM 1

DIAGRAM 2

NOTES

DIAGRAM 1

DIAGRAM 2

NOTES

DIAGRAM 1

DIAGRAM 2

NOTES

DIAGRAM 1

DIAGRAM 2

NOTES

GAME STATISTICS

DATE:_____ OPPONENT: _____ H/A

	1ST QTR	2ND QTR	3RD QTR	FINAL
US				
OPPONENT				

PLAYER	SOLO TACKLES	ASSISTS	TOTAL SACKS	QB SACKS	TACKLE LOSS	INT	FUMBLES CAUSED	FUMBLE RECOV.

PLAYER	SOLO TACKLES	ASSISTS	TOTAL SACKS	QB SACKS	TACKLE LOSS	INT	FUMBLES CAUSED	FUMBLE RECOV.

DIAGRAM 1

DIAGRAM 2

NOTES

DIAGRAM 1

DIAGRAM 2

NOTES

DIAGRAM 1

DIAGRAM 2

NOTES

DIAGRAM 1

DIAGRAM 2

NOTES

GAME STATISTICS

DATE:_____ OPPONENT: _____ H/A

	1ST QTR	2ND QTR	3RD QTR	FINAL
US				
OPPONENT				

PLAYER	SOLO TACKLES	ASSISTS	TOTAL SACKS	QB SACKS	TACKLE LOSS	INT	FUMBLES CAUSED	FUMBLE RECOV.

PLAYER	SOLO TACKLES	ASSISTS	TOTAL SACKS	QB SACKS	TACKLE LOSS	INT	FUMBLES CAUSED	FUMBLE RECOV.

DIAGRAM 1

DIAGRAM 2

NOTES

DIAGRAM 1

DIAGRAM 2

NOTES

DIAGRAM 1

DIAGRAM 2

NOTES

DIAGRAM 1

DIAGRAM 2

NOTES

GAME STATISTICS

DATE:_____   OPPONENT: _____   H/A

	1ST QTR	2ND QTR	3RD QTR	FINAL
US				
OPPONENT				

PLAYER	SOLO TACKLES	ASSISTS	TOTAL SACKS	QB SACKS	TACKLE LOSS	INT	FUMBLES CAUSED	FUMBLE RECOV.

PLAYER	SOLO TACKLES	ASSISTS	TOTAL SACKS	QB SACKS	TACKLE LOSS	INT	FUMBLES CAUSED	FUMBLE RECOV.
PLAYER	SOLO TACKLES	ASSISTS	TOTAL SACKS	QB SACKS	TACKLE LOSS	INT	FUMBLES CAUSED	FUMBLE RECOV.

DIAGRAM 1

DIAGRAM 2

NOTES

DIAGRAM 1

DIAGRAM 2

NOTES

DIAGRAM 1

DIAGRAM 2

NOTES

DIAGRAM 1

DIAGRAM 2

NOTES

GAME STATISTICS

DATE:_____   OPPONENT: _____   H/A

	1ST QTR	2ND QTR	3RD QTR	FINAL
US				
OPPONENT				

PLAYER	SOLO TACKLES	ASSISTS	TOTAL SACKS	QB SACKS	TACKLE LOSS	INT	FUMBLES CAUSED	FUMBLE RECOV.

PLAYER	SOLO TACKLES	ASSISTS	TOTAL SACKS	QB SACKS	TACKLE LOSS	INT	FUMBLES CAUSED	FUMBLE RECOV.

DIAGRAM 1

DIAGRAM 2

NOTES

DIAGRAM 1

DIAGRAM 2

NOTES

DIAGRAM 1

DIAGRAM 2

NOTES

DIAGRAM 1

DIAGRAM 2

NOTES

GAME STATISTICS

DATE:_____   OPPONENT: _____ H/A

	1ST QTR	2ND QTR	3RD QTR	FINAL
US				
OPPONENT				

PLAYER	SOLO TACKLES	ASSISTS	TOTAL SACKS	QB SACKS	TACKLE LOSS	INT	FUMBLES CAUSED	FUMBLE RECOV.

PLAYER	SOLO TACKLES	ASSISTS	TOTAL SACKS	QB SACKS	TACKLE LOSS	INT	FUMBLES CAUSED	FUMBLE RECOV.
PLAYER	SOLO TACKLES	ASSISTS	TOTAL SACKS	QB SACKS	TACKLE LOSS	INT	FUMBLES CAUSED	FUMBLE RECOV.

DIAGRAM 1

DIAGRAM 2

NOTES

DIAGRAM 1

DIAGRAM 2

NOTES

DIAGRAM 1

DIAGRAM 2

NOTES

DIAGRAM 1

DIAGRAM 2

NOTES

GAME STATISTICS

DATE:_____ OPPONENT: _____ H/A

	1ST QTR	2ND QTR	3RD QTR	FINAL
US				
OPPONENT				

PLAYER	SOLO TACKLES	ASSISTS	TOTAL SACKS	QB SACKS	TACKLE LOSS	INT	FUMBLES CAUSED	FUMBLE RECOV.

PLAYER	SOLO TACKLES	ASSISTS	TOTAL SACKS	QB SACKS	TACKLE LOSS	INT	FUMBLES CAUSED	FUMBLE RECOV.
PLAYER	SOLO TACKLES	ASSISTS	TOTAL SACKS	QB SACKS	TACKLE LOSS	INT	FUMBLES CAUSED	FUMBLE RECOV.

DIAGRAM 1

DIAGRAM 2

NOTES

DIAGRAM 1

DIAGRAM 2

NOTES

DIAGRAM 1

DIAGRAM 2

NOTES

DIAGRAM 1

DIAGRAM 2

NOTES

GAME STATISTICS

DATE:_____   OPPONENT: _____   H/A

	1ST QTR	2ND QTR	3RD QTR	FINAL
US				
OPPONENT				

PLAYER	SOLO TACKLES	ASSISTS	TOTAL SACKS	QB SACKS	TACKLE LOSS	INT	FUMBLES CAUSED	FUMBLE RECOV.

PLAYER	SOLO TACKLES	ASSISTS	TOTAL SACKS	QB SACKS	TACKLE LOSS	INT	FUMBLES CAUSED	FUMBLE RECOV.
PLAYER	SOLO TACKLES	ASSISTS	TOTAL SACKS	QB SACKS	TACKLE LOSS	INT	FUMBLES CAUSED	FUMBLE RECOV.

DIAGRAM 1

DIAGRAM 2

NOTES

DIAGRAM 1

DIAGRAM 2

NOTES

CPSIA information can be obtained
at www.ICGtesting.com
Printed in the USA
LVHW060241041219
639376LV00012B/366/P